Mr. Darcy

Elizabeth

Mr. Bingley

Jane

Plate 1

The Bennets Attend Church

Mrs. B

Glue to back of Mrs. Bennet's bonnet

leave open

do not cut out white space between arm and body

Ly

E

J

Plate 2

D

B

E

J

Cut slit at edge
of Elizabeth's hand;
insert fan

Cut slit at top
of Jane's hand;
insert fan

Plate 3

W

Lady Catherine
meets Elizabeth

LC

do not cut out
white space between
arms and body

Mrs. B

Ly

Mr. Wickham joins
the militia

Lydia at home

Mrs. Bennet
at home

Plate 4

D

Mr. Darcy writes to
Elizabeth

E

Elizabeth walks
to Nevelfield

do not cut out
white space between
arm and body

B

do not cut out
white space between
arm and body

Mr. Bingley
at Nevelfield

place tab
behind face

J

Jane rides to
Nevelfield

Plate 5

Dinner at Rosings

leave
open

glue to back of
Lady Catherine's bonnet

W

LC

Ly

Mr. Wickham's
dress uniform

Mrs. B

Lydia and
Mrs. Bennet at
the Assembly Ball

Plate 6

D

B

Mr. Bingley
at home

E

J

Mr. Darcy
at home

Elizabeth writing letters

Jane receives a letter

Plate 7

place tab
behind face

Lady
Catherine
attends
church

leave open

glue to back of
Lady Catherine's bonnet

D

LC

E

J

Mr. Darcy at
Nevelfield

Elizabeth visits Pemberly

Jane visits London

Plate 8

leave open

glue to back of
Lydia's bonnet

glue to back of
Mrs. Bennet's hat

leave open

Ly

Mrs. B

E

J

Lydia shops for
clothes in London

Mrs. Bennet, Elizabeth,
and Jane in the garden
at Longbourne

Plate 9

W

Mr. Wickham has tea
at Longbourne

Lady Catherine
confronts Elizabeth

leave open

glue to back of
Lady Catherines's hat

LC

Ly

Lydia trims a bonnet

Mrs. B

Mrs. Bennet takes tea

Plate 10

B

place tab behind face

do not cut out
white space
between arm
and body

Lydia elopes with
Mr. Wickham

Ly

J

Mr. Bingley takes
a stroll

E

Elizabeth
dines at Rosings

Jane returns
from London

Plate 11

Lady Catherine takes
tea alone

W

LC

glue to back of
Mrs. Bennet's
bonnet

leave open

glue to back of
Lydia's bonnet

leave open

Ly

Mrs. B

Mr. Wickham returns
with his bride

Mrs. Lydia Wickham

Mother of the brides

Plate 12

D

B

E

J

cut slit at
top of Elizabeth's
hand, fold
down tab and
insert it
into the slit

cut slit at top
of Jane's hand,
fold down tab
and insert it
into the slit

Plate 13